MONSTER MANNERS

At Mealtimes

Written by
Charis Mather

Designed by
Amy Li

This edition is published by arrangement with BookLife Publishing

Library of Congress Control Number:
2024953063

ISBN
979-8-89359-329-7 (library bound)
979-8-89359-413-3 (paperback)
979-8-89359-384-6 (epub)
979-8-89359-359-4 (hosted ebook)

Printed in the United States of America
Mankato, MN
092025

sales@northstareditions.com
888-417-0195

Written by:
Charis Mather

Edited by:
Rebecca Phillips-Bartlett

Designed by:
Amy Li

PHOTO CREDITS
All images are courtesy of Shutterstock.com, unless otherwise specified. With thanks to Getty Images, Thinkstock Photo and iStockphoto.

Recurring – Agafonov Oleg, Archiwiz, Curly Pat, Omeris, Dedraw Studio. P3 – natchapohn. P8 – Line-of-thought.

Monsters know many things.

They know how to cook and how to clean...

They know how to go shopping and how to look after pets...

But there is one thing that many monsters do not know...

MANNERS!

Tickles and Pod were excited. Tonight, Gram Gram was coming to visit while Mama and Papa were out. Gram Gram always made the best meals. Tickles licked her lips.

Thinking about Gram Gram's food made Tickles's tummy rumble. The funny noise made her little brother laugh. Then his tummy rumbled, too!

The monsters giggled. Then they heard a knock at the door.

"Did I hear a pair of grumbling tummies?" said a familiar voice.

An older monster poked her head into the room. "It must be nearly dinnertime."

"Gram Gram!" the little monsters squealed.

Tickles and Pod gave Gram Gram a big hug.

"Gram Gram, we were just thinking about your cooking," Tickles said. "You make the best mashed potatoes."

"Make us some mashed potatoes!" Pod said.

"Yes," said Tickles. "A giant bowl of mashed potatoes, as big as me!"

"We couldn't possibly eat that much mashed potatoes on our own," said Gram Gram.

"Mama and Papa can help us eat it," Pod said.

"We could set up a fancy meal for when they get back," Tickles suggested.

"That's a great idea," said Gram Gram. "But you will have to learn some mealtime manners first."

"Why don't you wash your hands? I'll set up the tea party table. Monsters with good manners have clean hands before they eat," said Gram Gram.

"Race you to the sink!" yelled Tickles, dashing out of the room. Pod ran out after her.

"Make sure to use soap!" Gram Gram called after them. Meanwhile, Gram Gram filled the teapot and put out the little plates, cups, and saucers. Then the children came back.

"Let's see those hands," Gram Gram said.

Pod and Tickles wiggled their clean fingers and giggled. Gram Gram smiled. "Wonderful. Now we are ready to eat."

Just then, Tickles's phone pinged. She checked her messages. "Look, Pod. Addy sent me a photo of her pet. He's so cute!"

"Tickles, please could you put that away while we eat?" Gram Gram said. "Monsters with good manners don't use their phones at the table."

"Of course, Gram Gram," said Tickles.

Gram Gram smiled and passed Tickles and Pod their teacups. "Thank you, Tickles. Not using your phone is a good way to show respect for the people you are eating with."

Tickles put her phone away. Then Pod reached over the table. He put all three muffins on his own plate.

"Pod, please could you share those muffins with us?" said Gram Gram. "Monsters with good manners make sure that everyone at the table gets a fair amount of food."

"Of course," Pod said. He passed Gram Gram and Tickles a muffin each.

"Thank you," said Gram Gram and Tickles.

Tickles took a big mouthful of muffin. "Mm, mm, mm," she said. "Monster muffins are delicious." As Tickles spoke, little pieces of muffin sprayed out of her mouth. Some crumbs landed on Pod.

"Ew!" said Pod, laughing. He spat a mouthful of crumbs back at his sister.

"FOOD FIGHT!" Tickles yelled.

She reached for more food to fling at Pod.

Quickly, Gram Gram moved the food out of their reach. "What a mess! Monsters with good manners do not play with their food."

"Oh," said the kids through mouthfuls of muffin crumbs. They looked at the table. "That did make quite a big mess. We should clean that up," Tickles said.

"That is a great idea," Gram Gram agreed. "Monsters with manners often offer to help out at mealtimes."

Together, Pod and Tickles cleaned up the crumbs. "Thank you, kids," Gram Gram said. "Let's pause our lessons on manners for now. Mama and Papa won't be long. I've got mashed potatoes to make."

"Yay!" the kids shouted.

Soon the house was filled with the wonderful smell of Gram Gram's mashed potatoes. Tickle and Pod heard keys jangling in the door. "They're back!" Tickles yelled.

"Mama and Papa are going to be so surprised when they see how good our manners are," Said Pod.

Pod was right. Mama and Papa were very surprised. Pod and Tickles ran off to wash their hands and put their phones away.

They were even more surprised when Pod offered to help Gram Gram dish out a fair amount of mashed potatoes to everyone at the table.

But Mama and Papa were most surprised when Pod and Tickles did not start a food fight during the meal.

"You really have learned your manners," Mama said, proud of her well-behaved little monsters.

"Not even one bit of mashed potatoes thrown," Papa said, amazed.

Tickles and Pod nodded. "Gram Gram taught us that food fights make a big mess," Tickles said.

"Well, what are we supposed to do with all of these leftover mashed potatoes now?" Papa wondered.

Tickles had an idea.

"I know someone who might have a better use for these leftovers than a food fight. Gram Gram, please may I send a message on my phone?"

"Just this once," Gram Gram agreed. "Thank you for checking with me first."

Quickly, Tickles sent out a message.

Not long later, there was a knock at the door. It was Addy and her lovely little pet.

Addy's pet smelled the delicious mashed potatoes right away. Before anyone could stop him, he jumped up onto the dinner table, right into the big bowl of leftovers!

Mashed potatoes went *everywhere!*

Not all monsters have good manners, but Tickles and Pod do. Do you?

Can you remember Gram Gram's mealtime manners?

- Wash your hands before eating.
- Put away your phones.
- Be fair when sharing food.
- Be helpful.
- Absolutely no playing with your food—if you can help it!